Bats Balls & Altar Calls

BOB CRAM

Bats Balls & Altar Calls

David B. Smith

Pacific Press Publishing Association
Boise, Idaho
Oshawa, Ontario, Canada

Edited by Marvin Moore
Designed by Tim Larson
Cover illustration by Lars Justinen
Inside illustrations by Bob Cram
Type set in 10/12 Century Schoolbook

The author assumes full responsibility for the accuracy of all
facts and quotations as cited in this book.

Library of Congress Catalog Card Number: 87-62340

ISBN 0-8163-0753-9

87 88 89 90 91 • 5 4 3 2 1

Contents

Dedication

This book is lovingly dedicated to my wife Lisa and my daughters Kami and Karli, who patiently endured as I watched literally hundreds of baseball games on television in painstaking research for this manuscript.

Chapter 1
Opening Day

Opening Day. What a beautiful ring that has to it!

I don't really start looking forward to the new baseball season with real anticipation until about the first of February. By the time I've watched or listened to 162 regular-season games, plus playoffs and the World Series in October, I'm ready for a few months off. So is my wife Lisa, who currently serves as vice-president of the Los Angeles chapter of Baseball Widows Anonymous.

Then, of course, there's football and basketball. Between the two, I make it through the end of January without any trouble.

Then in February I begin getting restless again. I switch the car radio from FM to AM in preparation for the coming season. I start exercising my wrist so I can quickly turn the TV knob back and forth between channels for those days when two games are on at the same time. I begin topping off my gas tank at the local service station every other day, just to see if the new season's baseball schedules are in yet.

The exhibition schedule begins in March, but those games really don't count for anything, except to Orioles' manager Earl Weaver. I listen to them, to be sure, but not with any real fervor. Nothing really matters until opening day.

I'm sure the players approach the opening of the season with a sense of anticipation as well. Think of it. Every player begins the year from the same starting point. Each hitter starts the season with a clean slate. Every pitcher in the league steps onto the mound with no earned runs against him. All twenty-six teams begin the season with identical records and no deficits in the "games behind" column.

What an opportunity! I've always envied the Cincinnati Reds, who traditionally open the new season. Because they start one day before most of the other teams, the Reds, by winning that opening game, can immediately vault into first place! They can lead the pack by a full half-game before anyone else even shows up at the ballpark.

Of course, the converse is also true: they nose dive straight into the cellar if they lose game one.

Hitters face the pleasant prospect of being able to start the year off with a perfect 1.000 batting average. I remember well the beginning of the 1980 season. The Dodgers opened the year in Houston's Astrodome. The leadoff hitter for Houston, on the very first pitch from L.A.'s Burt Hooton, whistled a homer over the left field wall.

What a beginning! Batting a thousand! A perfect slugging percentage! The league led in home runs with one.

Poor Burt Hooton, on the other hand, was saddled momentarily with an ERA of *infinity*. Ouch! One run allowed divided by zero innings officially pitched.

I've always wondered whether a newspaper would ever have the gall to list a pitcher's earned run average as "infinity." The answer is Yes. In the 1981 World Series game four, between the Dodgers and the Yankees, Bob Welch began the game for L.A., and gave up several runs without recording a single out. The *San Francisco Chronicle* dutifully recorded him as the starting pitcher, and under the ERA column they brazenly listed it: "inf."

Batters will sometimes create a little suspense by getting several hits to begin the year. Couple that early hitting streak with a few walks and sacrifice bunts, and a lucky player may still be at the perfect 1.000 mark after several games have gone by. By the same token, a good pitcher may go three or four games without giving up an earned run. One month into the campaign, he may still be sporting an unblemished 0.00 ERA.

Sooner or later, however, every player falls from grace. All it takes is one out, and the 1.000 average is gone forever. No hitting streak in the world can restore it to its original state of perfection. And all a pitcher needs is one earned run charged to his account to make the perfect zero ERA forever a thing of the past. It's just like a 4.0 GPA: one B and it's over.

I'm sure many batters and pitchers, at some point in the season, wish they could have a fresh start. A hitter struggling through a protracted slump might welcome the opportunity to begin anew rather than struggle to inch the suffering average up for the remainder of the season.

And the same is true of the team as a whole. So many lofty goals and spring-training fantasies inevitably bite the dust. Only four teams can be in first place in their respective divisions. The others either plot comeback strategies or announce to the press that they are in a "rebuilding phase."

I imagine those twenty-two clubs would probably be relieved if baseball commissioner Peter Ueberroth were to unexpectedly announce: "Listen, we got off to a bad start. The season just isn't going like we hoped it would. Effective July 1, we're beginning again. All teams are right back at the starting gate with a 0-0 mark."

Wiping the slate clean. Opening day. Forgiveness. A new beginning.

Baseball is a lot like life. Humanity craves a new beginning too!

Have you ever gotten yourself into a mess so overwhelming that you simply couldn't see a way to get through it? Have you ever made a series of blunders or misjudgments so horrible, and with such awful impact, that you couldn't bear to think of the possible outcome?

What a temptation it is to cry out at that moment for a new beginning! "If I could only start over," you plead. "Let me backtrack to the beginning of this nightmare and take a new direction. Give me a clean slate."

It's at moments like these that the forgiving power of the gospel really is good news! Forgiveness is yours for the asking! The worst stains of sin can be instantly blotted out.

It doesn't matter how deep your involvement. It doesn't matter how bad the crime. Even the longest, vilest string of violations can be instantly wiped away.

At the lowest possible moment of your "batting slump," you can look up and ask for a clean slate, a new start. God can grant the worst hitter in the league an opportunity to begin again, with no outs recorded on the scoresheet.

Yes, time and again, those precious words in 1 John 1:9 have given millions courage to go on with life: God "is faithful and just to forgive us our sins."

This doesn't mean God can instantly erase all the painful results of sin. We live in a universe governed by natural laws, and God can't negate them in order to cover up our mistakes. When the alcoholic cries out for forgiveness in his drunken stupor, God gladly forgives, but He doesn't usually take away the hangover. Long and difficult months of healing may still lie ahead.

A would-be burglar confesses his sinful state to God while being driven to the police station after an armed robbery. In the courts of heaven the slate is wiped clean. Down at the local precinct it's another matter. A price remains to be paid.

If you ask God for a new beginning after years of infidelity and adultery, He will gladly forgive you, but your road to marital recovery may be an arduous path of counseling and hard work.

The promise of a new season doesn't carry with it a guarantee that the pitches will be any easier. It simply implies right standing with the Father. A new scoresheet. No more, no less.

And yet, along with the new start comes the promise of power. God's power. Philippians 4:13 contains our guarantee: "I can do all things through Christ which strengtheneth me." Help is available to right the wrongs. Divine assistance stands ready to repair the damage done, to mend broken hearts.

"My strength is sufficient for you," God assures us. He provides it all—the new start, and the power to make the new start work.

Do you need a new start? Ask for it. Today could be opening day for you.

Chapter 2
Flags and Crosses, Bread and Wine

Here's a trivia question that most baseball fans should be able to answer: What ritual does Davey Concepcion go through every time he comes up to bat for the Cincinnati Reds?

If you've seen many Cincinnati games, I know you've picked this one up. Davey always crosses himself after getting set in the batter's box.

Sometimes it works, and he gets a base hit. More often, however, my prayers cancel out his, since mine are usually on behalf of the other team, and he comes up empty.

Habits and superstitions are an integral part of the game of baseball. Various players have the little rites, the zany beliefs or routines they follow. I suspect that every team in the big leagues has at least one player with a Certified Flake diploma hanging in his locker.

I watched a batter once who went through the same little series of motions, not just upon stepping into the box, but between every pitch. Adjust the left batting glove. Then the right glove. Tug on cap. Wipe sweat off brow. Straighten wrist band. Hit bat against left shoe to knock out dirt. Then the right shoe. Tap bat on home plate. Pull on cap again. Give each glove one final tug. Ready to hit.

The entire routine took up to thirty seconds every time, and his at-bats seemed to go on forever. I used to be able to hop in my car just as he came to the plate, drive a mile and a half to Taco Bell, order my meal, drive back to the house, and he'd have a 2-1 count on him by then. Well, OK, maybe 2-2. I mean, he was really slow. People in the ballpark always planned their restroom breaks around him.

Sports fans, of course, can be just as nutty as the players. In his book *Paper Lion*, George Plimpton describes a football fan who discovered that whenever he drove to the ballpark taking a certain route, the team won. He developed a mania for driving there in a very particular manner, maintaining the same "lucky" speed, parking in the same spot each week, even wearing the same good-luck clothes every Sunday. It got to the point where he was counting his steps from the car to his lucky seat in the stadium, adding little adjustment "hops" if necessary, to make sure he didn't break the spell created by his package-plan approach.

All went well, of course, until the team went into an extended losing streak. The fan, plagued with guilt that he was somehow causing the skid, began frantically altering the routine. Side roads, new clothes, parking in a different lot, changing his seat assignment. He tried everything, looking for a new lucky combination. Nothing helped, and the team finished in the cellar. Fortunately, they never found out where this fan lived or that he was responsible for their collective disintegration!

I'm not out to be critical of a player's unique habits or rituals, especially if they happen to contain religious overtones. But I do sometimes wonder, especially in the case of a player like Concepcion, if such a gesture continues to have deep meaning over the years.

Davey crosses himself perhaps 500 times during a season. I don't know if he does it during the spring exhibition games or not. For all I know, he even does it in batting practice.

Does a prayer symbol like his, expressed 500 times a year, season after season, continue to have the meaning it is intended to have? Does it always represent a deep inward attitude of worship? Or has it become just a meaningless ritual that long ago lost its significance?

Only Concepcion knows the answer to that one. But human experience is that symbols can very easily become hollow and mechanical. They can quickly lose their intended impact.

Take the American flag, for instance. Just a simple piece of cloth with some stripes and stars on it. Red, white, and blue fabric. Yet this ordinary cloth represents something that millions of Americans have unhesitatingly paid for with their lives. And if I asked you straight out, most of you would indicate a willingness to give your life for your country, for the ideals and heritage represented by that simple piece of fabric.

The signers of the Declaration of Independence, in affixing their names to that document, pledged their homes, their resources, their sacred honor, and their very lives in defense of what our flag represented. Some of them gladly forfeited all those things for the new cause of liberty. Yet this magnificent symbol can so easily become trivialized. It's possible to become jaded, to lose the spirit of patriotism and loyalty that our flag is meant to create. After a while, if you're not careful, you can end up seeing only the cloth and not the ideals represented by the red, white, and blue.

What a tragedy it is when the flag ceases to inspire! When it no longer reminds us of the sacrifices that made this country possible. How sad when we can see the flag, and sing our national anthem, yet fail to recognize the significance of our country's heritage.

This is one symbol that has great potential to inspire, to define loyalty, to restore patriotism . . . but only if we allow it to.

The Christian faith is rich in symbolism, filled with tools of inspiration and faith, reminders that serve to stimulate thought and create an attitude of spiritual surrender.

We put crosses on our church steeples and hymnals. We partake of communion bread and wine. We are baptized by water into the fellowship of the church. In some faiths, members wash each other's feet, as our Lord did before His last supper with His disciples.

These symbols have great power to change hearts. They can be a true education for Christians, reminding us of things that are eternal.

Or they can become empty rituals. Bread and wine can become just calories. Tiny gold crosses can become mere jewelry.

It's up to us.

I invite you to allow the Christian symbols to work in your life. Give them the opportunity to make the impact they were intended to have.

That requires a commitment to the art of thoughtfulness. It demands a willingness to slow down, to be reflective. But the rewards are well worth it.

So when you partake of the bread and wine or are a part of the beautiful ritual of baptism or experience the stark appeal of the cross of Christ, let it count for something. Think of what these symbols mean to you personally. Give them time to stir your heart and renew your commitment. The next time you step into the batter's box or meet other life crises large or small, make sure that with the symbol of prayer comes the prayer itself—and, hopefully, a base hit too!

Chapter 3
Tape Delay

One of my great pet peeves is students who ask a teacher a question to which he doesn't know the answer. It's especially irritating when the teacher's me.

One standard method of coping with this situation is to launch into a long and very convoluted tirade designed to confuse and intimidate the student. Throwing in some big words like *pulchritudinous* or *perspicacity* is generally effective as well.

Another generally reliable technique is to roll one's eyes heavenward as if to imply that everyone in the western hemisphere over the age of two and a half knows the answer to *that* one. If that doesn't get the student to withdraw the question, I proceed to Plan C: announce a fire drill. Very seldom will I look him straight in the eye and calmly reply, "I have no idea." But every now and then, I do like to surprise kids with the unexpected.

I was deep in a discussion with my tenth grade religion class one day (I was teaching in a Christian school at the time) when a thoughtful student tossed me one of those hand-grenade questions. "Does God already know who's going to be saved and who's going to be lost?"

"Hmmmmmm. Yes, I suppose so," I replied confidently. "He knows the past and the future."

So far so good. But then came the follow-up.

"Does He try hard to save even those He knows aren't going to make it?"

19

I thought for a moment. Actually several moments. "Well, uh, yes, I guess He must. He sends the Holy Spirit to work on every person's heart. Wouldn't be fair, otherwise, right?"

The student then zipped two quick strikes by me. "Why should the Holy Spirit waste His time trying to save people He knows aren't going to make it anyway? And *if* He spends time on them, how does He put any enthusiasm into it?"

Aren't those great questions? I have to admit I was so impressed I didn't even bother to try ducking them. I looked him right in the eye and replied, "Larry, you got me on both of these. I honestly don't have a good answer for you, but let's both do some thinking about it and see what we come up with."

How *does* God put forth a legitimate effort to save those who will not be saved? As I thought about it later, my mind went back to The Great Tape Delay Deception.

It happened on a Monday evening back in '79. I was up in northern California visiting my parents for a few weeks during my summer teaching break. Returning to their home after running an errand late in the afternoon, I came across a ballgame on the car radio. One of the teams was the San Francisco Giants. Since I follow the exploits of Bay Area teams with only mild interest, I didn't pay a lot of attention to the sportscaster's running account of the game.

Suddenly I realized that I was listening to a game that was going to be on the ABC Monday Night Game of the Week later that evening. For the convenience of West Coast viewers, the game was going to be televised as a tape delay, allowing baseball fans to see the entire game after getting home from work.

The radio broadcast, of course, was live. A quick glance at my watch showed that there was going to be about a four-inning gap between the two. An evil plan began to formulate in my mind. Listening intently now, I soon heard a rather unusual baseball sequence. With two outs, the team at bat came up with four consecutive singles, followed by a long foul ball, and then an enormous home run.

"Four singles, long foul ball, enormous home run, bottom of

the fifth," I rehearsed to myself several times, wickedly plotting my deception.

The plan worked simply enough. We sat down to supper, which I devoured quickly with one eye on the clock.

"Isn't there a game on tonight, Dad?" I remarked casually, as I finished my dessert. "It's Monday night, you know. OK if I turn it on?"

He grunted a response that I interpreted to mean, "Why, certainly! I've been looking forward all day to watching this game."

You'll have to understand that my dad watches ballgames only under extreme family pressure to "be sociable" and often takes copies of the *Reader's Digest* or his Greek lexicon (he's a preacher) to read at the ballpark whenever we plan an outing.

I found the right channel, settled back, and impatiently waited for the big inning to roll around.

Finally it came. "Come on, Dad, pay attention," I teased, kicking his copy of *Two Hundred and Fifty Tips on Installing Bathroom Plumbing* out of his hand and across the room. "This is a crucial game."

He didn't bother to point out that very few games played in June could be labeled as crucial, especially if they involved the San Francisco Giants, but he did sit up and begin to watch.

As I knew they would, the first two batters meekly struck out. "Come on, do something," I moaned, with a touch a theatrics. "We need a hit right now."

Bingo. Base hit up the middle.

"Now you're paying attention," I cried at the TV, looking sidelong at my dad to see if he had noticed my effectiveness. "How about an encore? One more base hit coming up?"

"Nah," my dad snorted. "No way."

Bingo. Base hit number two.

"Hello, what's this?" I exclaimed. "They *are* listening to me now."

I began to get carried away. "Base hit to left right now will bring that run home."

No sooner said than done. "Base hit to left, and the run is home," intoned the announcer, copying my style.

"Here comes another one," I predicted with emotion ringing in my voice. "Four for four!"

Base hit. Four straight lucky guesses and a two-out two-run rally.

Dad looked around nervously. "What's going on here, anyway?"

"Nothing," I chortled. "I just got the vibes, that's all. I'll bet you a buck we get a home run right now."

Dad glanced around the living room to see if any parishioners were present. "I better not," he concluded. "You must be on to something."

Suddenly I was hit by cosmic vibrations that rattled the whole couch. "Here comes a fly ball, *deep to left*, but foul." Sure enough.

"Now the home run," I predicted. "Make it six perfect picks in a row, batter!" The ball obligingly sailed over the fence as my dad sailed right out of his easy chair.

"That's it!" he bellowed. "Either you're in league with evil forces, or we're watching some kind of rerun here. Now confess before I send you home."

Between gales of laughter I denied any complicity. "Face it, Dad," I chortled. "I could make a living at this."

As far as I recall, I never did tell him the truth.

There's a point to the story, of course. There are lessons to be learned from almost anything in life, even a videotaped baseball game.

If you ever have the experience of seeing a game "live," and then later watching that same game on video tape, I think you may get just a glimpse of what God goes through with us.

For one thing, you're helpless to change the outcome of the game. Players strike out or drop balls in the game, and later on the tape they do it again. And there isn't much point in shouting at the TV, "Hang onto it this time," or, "Oh, no, here comes that grand slam again!"

You can see the plays coming, but you can't change them.

What would it be like, I've wondered at times, if I could see videotapes, not of yesterday's games, but of *tomorrow's* contests?

Eerie thought. Imagine the experience of watching tomorrow's game on TV, then going to that same game in person, and seeing events transpire in front of you that you already know are going to take place.

Except for the possibility of making a very handsome living at the expense of unsuspecting bookmakers, I don't think I'd like it much. Especially if I couldn't change the results by giving the manager advice. For example: "Don't pitch to Mike Schmidt tonight, Lasorda. Would you believe, two homers and five RBIs?" Or how about, "Don't even get off the team bus, guys. Unless you really *want* to get creamed 14-1 and make five errors in the fourth inning."

How does God handle it? How does He watch our lives unfold day after day, knowing full well where we're going to blow it, knowing with complete certainty exactly which people are never going to respond to Him?

I think we have to recognize, first of all, that He doesn't write out the game Himself, inning by inning. He watches the game, to be sure, but He doesn't dictate who's going to win and who's going to lose. *Knowing* what's going to happen doesn't mean He *makes* it happen.

As far as working with all His power and enthusiasm to save the unsavable is concerned, I'd like to offer up three theories. I'll let you guess which one is my favorite.

First, I believe God makes every attempt to save everybody, because that's the only fair thing to do, and being fair is simply part of the character of God.

When I was an algebra teacher, I had an obligation to work equally hard to help all students pass, even though I knew with certainty that some would fail. Many times I knew with reasonable certainty, before the first day of school was over, *which* students were going to flunk. Nevertheless, as a professional educator, I was compelled to give the doomed pupils every advantage that the most gifted students received. To do otherwise would have been unjust.

Second, and this is a related thought, we could perhaps conclude that God is interested in how the universe perceives Him. Can you imagine the response from the rest of the angels if God, knowing that some poor sinner wasn't going to make it anyway, simply abandoned him to his eventual fate?

We would complain, and rightly so, that God was not only predicting the future but writing it as well. Just like the flunking algebra student who comes up to me during parent-teacher conferences, jabs his finger in my face, and charges: "You didn't give me any help! That's why I flunked."

My protests that I didn't bother to help him *because* I knew he was going to flunk would fall on deaf and angry ears, wouldn't they? I'd have left myself wide open to a charge of mathematical predestination.

Neither does God want to be accused of condemning people to be lost simply because He knows their futures and the eventual results of their decisions. If there's one thing God wants us to understand, it's that every person who ever lived has been free to be saved, or free to be lost. Christ's sacrifice has made the gift of salvation available to everyone; indeed, it's God's plan that all be saved. Remember? God is "not willing that any should perish." 2 Peter 3:9.

God is determined that no behavior on His part shall ever take away from our free power of choice in this matter of salvation. And His omniscient knowledge of the future no more takes away our freedom than does my presence today at the ballgame I saw yesterday on my futuristic "Tomorrow's Ballgame" videotape.

So God works tirelessly to reach the unreachable, and the Holy Spirit labors in love for those who will never respond, out of divine fairness and an ultimate commitment to the preservation of free choice and self-determined destinies.

Those are two theories. I think they're not too bad, except that they perhaps cast God in a rather self-serving light. God is fair, of course; yet I think there's more to this than a desire on His part to avoid universal criticism on grounds of unfairness or favoritism.

No, God is bigger than that. There's something larger and more generous behind His efforts. Consider the possibility that God continues to work tirelessly for those He knows will never make it for one very simple and basic reason:

He loves them so very much that He simply cannot help Himself.

Can you relate to that? God loves people so much that even when He reads their final chapter and sees they will not be saved, He simply cannot give them up. Up until the very last moment, He continues to reach out to them with love in His heart and, I'm sure, tears of frustration in His eyes.

Just like the young man who continues to send love letters and boxes of candy to the girl who has vehemently rejected him, God's love compels Him to court sinners right up until that final moment of divine anguish when, out of respect for human free will, He must reluctantly let them go.

What a God! Inscrutably fair? Yes. Concerned about freedom of choice and free will, and maybe even His universal reputation? I think so. Yet motivated most of all by a bigness of character and a wellspring of love that flies in the face of human logic.

A love like that defies hopelessness. It refuses to accept defeat. Most of all, it creates a response. Maybe it even rewrites destiny once in a while.

Chapter 4
Batting Crowns or World Series Rings

"He's a team player."

Most managers will tell you that's the highest tribute a baseball star can receive. A player who puts the team's success ahead of his own personal goals or triumphs is a valuable commodity.

Baseball is a game filled with team plays. Selfless contributions can often mean the difference between victory and defeat.

The most obvious example, of course, is the sacrifice bunt, where a player deliberately makes an out in order to move another runner into scoring position. Bottom of the ninth, tied score, leadoff batter walks, next hitter bunts him to second base, third batter singles up the middle, the game's over. The sacrifice sets up the whole thing.

Other team plays aren't so obvious, but still an integral part of the game. One of them is executed by the batter who, with nobody out, successfully hits the ball to the right side of the infield so that a runner can go from second to third and set up the "sacrifice fly" score. He tries for a hit, of course, but he may alter his regular swing in order to keep the ball away from the shortstop or third baseman. The attempt even counts against his average if he makes an out, so it truly is an unselfish play. Sportscasters always offer high praise for a player who successfully "moves his man along" this way. "The ballplayer's play," they call it.

Swinging at bad pitches on the hit-and-run play is another

example. A batter may make an out swinging at a pitch he would otherwise let go by, but if he makes contact and avoids the double play, he succeeds in unselfishly moving the base runner up a notch. Again, a team player's play. For years, Steve Garvey has been known as just such a team player, swinging at dozens of junk pitches on hit-and-run plays during the course of a season. Amazingly, his batting average has always been right up there with the league's top ten despite his role as a team player.

Other sports also have their players who fill team roles. Not everyone in pro football, for instance, can be a quarterback, wide receiver, or field goal specialist. The game also needs its blockers and guards, many of whom play their entire careers in relative anonymity.

Former Green Bay guard Jerry Kramer, in his book *Instant Replay*, wrote with mock bitterness about completing his entire career without scoring a single touchdown. Yet, in the unforgettable divisional playoff against Dallas in 1967, it was Kramer who made the big block at the goal line that allowed quarterback Bart Starr to slip through for the winning touchdown.

Just about any player, whether in professional sports or on a local church softball league, experiences a certain conflict between a desire for team accomplishment and personal glory. Contributing to a team win is important, of course. Yet there's something very compelling about protecting one's own batting average.

I remember a softball game where my team won big. We scored twenty runs, with all my teammates racking up base hits. But my personal line score read 0-for-4. I hit into a double play and left about seven runners on base all by myself. Everyone else was celebrating, but I felt miserable.

In another game, I could do no wrong. Five-for-five at the plate, including a double, plus a walk and a flock of RBIs. In the field I made several sparkling plays. We lost the game by one run, but I drove home feeling pretty good.

It's so very human to care more about our personal achievements than about the good of the team. "It doesn't matter how

the team comes out as long as I do well." That's not how it should be, of course. The struggle is greatest, I suppose, for a player who is benched in favor of someone else. Talk about conflicting emotions! It takes a pretty unselfish player to "sit on the pine" and root for the person who's out there playing your position because the manager thinks he's better.

This conflict between team goals and personal success is always heightened whenever a player is closing in on some milestone. The media hype and fan attention are unavoidable, I suppose. Still, there's something about the quest for these personal goals that is somehow contrary to the larger team spirit of the game.

There's really nothing wrong with a pitcher's trying hard to get career win number 300, or for a player's attempting to capture the stolen base crown. But it's a little disappointing when these campaigns to get into the record books almost rewrite the way the game is played.

I remember Steve Garvey's consecutive-game streak of a few years ago. Now, I'll be the first to defend Steve as one who cared more about playing every day so he could contribute to the team's success than he did about a niche in the record books. Still, there was something a little bit artificial about the whole thing. Steve would be deathly ill, with a temperature of 103°, but still come in and play one inning. Or he would be in the middle of a horrible slump that would have put any other player on the bench or even on the bus back to the Triple-A club in Albuquerque. But because of the ongoing streak, Steve would come in for one at-bat, strike out, and go sit back down. The streak seemed to have become the tail that wagged the dog.

It was the same story when Rickey Henderson was gunning for the stolen-base record a few years back. In the late innings of the final game of a homestand in Oakland, Rickey reached first successfully, and was all set up to break the record, except for one thing: second base was already occupied by another player. To almost nobody's surprise, the base runner on second just happened to wander too far off the bag and got picked off! This opened up the base, giving Rickey one more opportunity to set the mark in front of the home crowd. The base runner and manager, Billy Martin, claimed innocence, but fans and sportswriters alike were dubious.

Almost any ballplayer in the game, whether superstar or utility player, jealously guards one thing: his batting average. That number, more than any other, spells the difference between success and failure, between Cadillacs and late-model Fords.

In fact, it's said that most big leaguers develop their peripheral vision by glancing out of the corner of their eye at the scoreboard to see if their just-completed at-bat is scored as a base hit or an error. Former catcher Bob Uecker, who scrambled his entire career just to get his average up to .200, describes his technique.

"After I reach first base, I just reach down as if to pick up a handful of dirt. You know, to rub between my palms. Then, as I straighten up, I can glance up at the scoreboard without anyone seeing me look."

When asked if he always agreed with the official scorer, Bob interjected: "Well, if I get on base, I count it as a hit. If I walk, I count that too. Anything I hit good, I count."

"What are you batting right now, by your own calculations?"

"About .750."

Players don't seem mindful of the fact that getting on base on an error or a walk makes just as big a contribution to the team as does a clean single. No, the three percentage points added to the average are too often the all-important factor.

World Series rings. Super Bowl trophies. Stanley Cups. These, rather than Golden Gloves or Cy Young Award trophies, are the team rewards that ought to be first and foremost in a player's mind. Every play, every accomplishment, every success, every record broken, should be directed toward the goal of team victory.

Jesus once told a story that, in a roundabout kind of way, talks about team victory. You remember the parable of the landowner who recruited people to work in his vineyard. He hired some workers first thing in the morning, others later on in the day, and still others about an hour before quitting time.

At the end of the day, however, he paid the whole crowd exactly the same. Which was great for the newest arrivals, but more than a little irritating for the tired-and-sweaty crew that started at sunrise.

Now, looking at this story from a workman's point of view, you'd have to say this entrepreneur wasn't a very satisfactory employer. His it's-my-money-to-do-with-as-I-please attitude does very little to establish harmonious labor relations among the pickers.

But perhaps there is a lesson for ballplayers. And maybe one for Christians too. The fact is, the harvest came in. The overriding goal was accomplished. The championship was won. And if some workers made more than others, or had better batting averages, so what?

"Don't worry so much about what's happening in the lives of others," Jesus says. "You keep your bargain with Me, and things will be all right for you. You may make a little more or a little less than others in this life. Perhaps you'll be famous; perhaps not. But if you labor in My vineyard, eternal life will be yours."

It's a hard lesson to learn. We're very conscious of our personal efforts as Christians. It's easy to point to a .975 church-attendance average or to compare our accomplishments with those of a less-successful church member. But, as this story points out, the wages at the end of the day are the same for everyone.

Even length of service doesn't seem to affect the final reward very much. The apostle Peter toiled for his Lord for years and years. At the end of his decades of faithful labor, how was he rewarded? Crucifixion. Upside-down, no less! On the other hand, how long did the thief on the cross serve Jesus? Maybe half an hour. Yet I imagine both of them will be perfectly content with their rewards in heaven.

John the Baptist was another team player. When his disciples complained about declining attendance at his evangelistic crusades, in contrast with the ever-growing popularity of Jesus' ministry, John replied simply, "He must increase, but I

must decrease." John 3:30. He understood and accepted his role, rejoicing in the triumphs of the gospel.

The prophet Daniel calmly turned down scarlet robes, a chain of gold, and the coveted "third ruler" rank in the world empire of Babylon, telling King Belshazzar to give them instead to someone else. His goal in life was to glorify the God of heaven before this heathen empire. Earthly reward held no attraction for him.

The list goes on. Moses could have been a king, but cast his lot with a team of losers instead. Christ could have come down off the cross and returned to His throne of honor in heaven, but He died for an ungrateful world. The apostle Paul, a candidate for a leading post in Israel's religious hierarchy, chose instead the hard life of a Christian missionary, declaring with conviction, "For to me to live is Christ." Philippians 1:21.

Somehow, when a person's mind is fixed on Christ and on the opportunity to spend an eternity with Him, the rewards and trophies and personal achievements of this life seem to fade. A concern for this team we call humanity overcomes a desire for individual recognition. In the words of the Christian hymn "Side by Side," "Heaven is our goal, to save every soul."

Let's make it there together, team.

Chapter 5
Standings

A few years ago my family and I decided to take a brief vacation in San Diego. "There's plenty to do in San Diego," we explained to the kids. "The zoo, Sea World, parks, motel swimming pool—lots of fun!"

As if the zoos and sea worlds and parks weren't enough, I made a remarkable discovery upon our arrival: The Los Angeles Dodgers were going to be in town for a three-game series with the Padres. In fact, the three games coincided perfectly with the exact three days we were planning to spend there on vacation.

I remarked to my wife, "It seems almost providential that the scheduling should work out like this. Here we are for three days, and the Dodgers are in town these same three days. And our motel is only two miles from the stadium!"

"What an incredible coincidence," my sweet wife observed, with more than a trace of cynical suspicion in her voice.

"You know," I went on, pretending not to notice her negative attitude, "it really does seem a shame not to take advantage of this chance to see some games. Usually, I have to drive three hours to see a ballgame. But here, I could practically walk to the stadium."

"Why don't you do just that?" she suggested.

"Why, thanks, Honey, I believe—"

"Walk to the stadium, that is."

Without going so far in relating this narrative that I put my wife in a really bad light, let me just say that after several hours of wheedling, long-term promises regarding housework duties, and a clause or two concerning new dresses purchased at San Diego's finest shops, I was happily on my way to the game.

I purchased a ticket, then made my way down to the box seats to sit right behind the dugout in the third row. Handsomely but inconspicuously dressed in a Dodger jacket, Dodger hat, and Dodger wristbands that had somehow found their way into my vacation gear, I settled back, took a sandwich out of my Dodger tote bag, and prepared to enjoy the game.

It wasn't long before I made a startling and rather disquieting discovery: Everyone at Jack Murphy Stadium hated me.

I couldn't understand it. To be sure, I wasn't wearing one of those unattractive Padre hats everyone else was sporting. And I didn't stand up on my chair and scream every time a Padre got lucky with a base hit.

But that still didn't justify the impolite remarks I was made to endure: catcalls regarding not only Dodger players but their fans, and me in particular, that included crude observations about Dodger abilities and ancestry, and a number of tasteless suggestions that I consider cutting short my vacation so I could go back where I came from.

The final straw came when the entire stadium crowd, 50,000 strong, began to chant in unison, "Dodgers #@*&%! Dodgers #@*&%! Dodgers #@*&%!"

Only by summoning my last ounces of willpower and bravado was I able to remain to the end of the game. I drove back to the motel shaken, vowing not to return to that hostile place for at least twenty-four hours.

It wasn't until our vacation had ended and I was safely back home that I was able to quietly reflect on this phenomenon of hatred I had experienced.

What is it that makes fans hate each other? I wondered. Why these bitter feelings toward a visiting team? What is it that inspires a fan to spend $1.25 to buy a full cup of beer just to dump on my head after a Dodger home run? This is a *game* we're talking about, not World War III.

I consoled myself with the thought that none of these expressions had been personal. My impeccably polite behavior certainly had done nothing to cause such outpourings of wrath as I had experienced. No, my misfortunes had been strictly guilt by association.

After a time, I finally hit upon the culprit: standings.

Standings, of course, are the comparative win-loss records of teams that put one club in first place, another in second, and so on. And when one club is perennially near the bottom of the stack, and in double figures in the "Games Behind" column in the sports pages, a certain amount of venom is generated against teams higher in the standings, and against the team in first place especially.

Let's face it. For years, the San Diego Padres had finished sixth in a field of six. (Oh for a return to those happy days.) And to constantly be not only in last place, but mathematically eliminated from the race by the middle of August, has a definitely harmful effect not only on a team's collective ego, but also on its general feelings of good will toward the teams higher up the ladder.

Naturally, the success of the Dodgers in recent years has made them the target for some of this San Diego emotion. Camaraderie between the two cities has largely evaporated, at least in the sports pages and the ballparks. Surely no one can deny that this poisonous ill will and hatred is bad for people. I heard a radio interview with a pitcher for the San Francisco Giants, another recent cellar dweller, where the question was asked, "What do you think of this Dodger team you're about to face?"

His answer was blunt and unhesitating: "I hate them, I hate them, I hate them."

What a stark testimony to the damaging effect of standings!

I have to wonder what would happen if the new commissioner of baseball, Peter Ueberroth, would courageously step forward and say, "We have to bring an end to this tide of animosity. This fist shaking, this anger, this hatred, this beer-pouring-on-heads has all got to stop."

What would be the result if he were to announce, during

the seventh inning stretch of a Monday night ABC game of the week, "By the power vested in me by the leagues, I am bringing to an end the existence of standings. From now on there will be no such thing as standings, win-loss records, 'games behind,' and first or last place"?

He continues: "In order to make this possible, we will henceforth not record wins and losses of teams. There will be no winners or losers. Players will no longer run the bases or try to score runs. ERAs and pitching records, batting averages and home run records, all divisive elements of the game, will now be a thing of the past.

"Let me hasten to add," he continues, "that this great institution we all love will continue. You fans keep coming to the ballparks every evening. These great players, these talented athletes, will put on a spectacular show of hitting, pitching, and fielding for you. They'll stage cooperative exhibitions that will still contain all the elements that make baseball the thrilling sport it is. Only the damaging win-at-all-costs mentality will be gone.

"Believe me," he concludes, "it's better this way."

Imagine it! No more fights. No more hurt feelings. No more selfish cries of, "We're Number One!" No more twinges of jealousy when reading the sports section that lists your team in last place.

What a paradise! No more hatred.

Unfortunately, we must also add, "No more fans." Because nobody will go to the ballpark anymore. Not this way.

Let's face it. People like hating the other team. People like screaming and throwing things. They like shouting, "Kill the umpire!" or, "Kill the manager!" or just, "Kill someone! Anyone!"

But the point still remains that by removing the standings, the comparisons, we also remove the hostility that divides us.

The last few years there's been a great deal of talk about "Star Wars" defensive space systems. The basic idea is that we develop space laser stations to destroy enemy nuclear missiles before they get close to our country. Without getting into the political pros and cons of such a proposal, let me ask you what the net effect would be if every nation on earth had access to the "Star Wars" system? What if every nation were completely invulnerable to incoming missiles?

One thing's for sure: Nations would soon stop building nuclear missiles, wouldn't they? In fact, with every nation on an equal basis, existing missiles could be relegated to the scrap heap or melted down into razor blades.

Worldwide SDI laser systems could end the era of powerful nations and weak nations, of superpowers and "satellite" countries. The great dividing barrier of nuclear threat would be gone. Each nation would be considered an equal, at least from a defense point of view.

By taking away nuclear might and the global tendency to have national "standings," we could eliminate some of the barriers of hostility that now exist.

In Ephesians 2:14, we read about a Person who breaks down barriers that divide people. "For he [Christ] is our peace, who has made us both one, and has broken down the dividing wall of hostility." RSV.

I don't have to tell you that when Jesus was here on earth, there was a "wall of hostility" between two groups: Jews and Gentiles. The barrier of anger and resentment boiled at a World Series level of emotion all year long. Yet Jesus effectively broke through that wall. The good news He came to give brought unity where there was once division. Former enemies worked side by side to spread His gospel. Persecutors became partners in the cause of Christ.

Is it possible that even today Jesus Christ could be the Power that tears down walls of hostility? Think for a moment about barriers that occur even among Christians. What causes them? More often than not, barriers are created by comparisons. By Christian "standings," if you will.

There are so many things that tempt us to compare. We look at another person's lifestyle and can't help but feel superior—or perhaps inferior. We notice how often someone is absent from church and subconsciously pat ourselves on the back for our perfect record. We see evidence that a person is struggling with sin, and we congratulate ourselves that we long ago won the victory over *that*. We use our twenty-twenty peripheral vision to note the amount someone else drops in the offering plate, and hope that the Lord notices how much more generous our contribution is.

Comparisons, comparisons. And all of them quietly, or perhaps not so quietly, creating barriers.

People often leave the church over such "standings." They expect the pastor to be perfect, and he isn't. So out the door they go. Some member, maybe even a church leader, makes a well-documented mistake, and we say to ourselves, "I can't associate with this. I'm leaving."

But think about this for a moment. Jesus can remove those barriers caused by comparisons. How? By making us all equal.

Let me ask you a question: How much do you deserve salvation—by yourself? For that matter, how much do any of us deserve it by ourselves? Not at all, right? I'm just as deserving as you: zero; and you're just as deserving as I am: also zero. Isaiah 64:6 reminds us that our righteousness is as "filthy rags." I don't know what filthy rags are going for on today's market, but this is one text that serves to keep us in our place!

You and I need to face the uncomfortable fact that we're really no more deserving of salvation than the most desperate criminals sitting on death row. In the eyes of God, and according to the standards of His law, we deserve death just as much as any one of them. In Ephesians 2:8, 9 we're reminded that none of us deserves salvation on our own. "It's the gift of God," Paul emphasizes. "It has nothing to do with your works, so don't do any ill-advised boasting." Each of us deserves to occupy last place in the standings of the league of heaven.

When you hold up my life or your life or anyone's life, to Christ's, we all come out the same. There's really no need for comparisons. We're all equal: completely worthless and undeserving.

"Well, thank you so much," I can hear you saying. "Stick to baseball stories, would you? What's the title of this book, anyway, *I'm Not OK, You're Not OK*"?

Let us hasten to examine the other side of this equality coin. When *I* accept Christ's perfect robe of righteousness,

and when *you* accept Christ's perfect robe of righteousness, what happens? Again, we're equal! Except that now we're both *totally* deserving of salvation. We're both completely accepted in the eyes of God. We're both stamped with the infinite price tags of His love.

Do you see why Jesus tears down barriers of hostility? Without Him, we're all the same, and with Him, we're all the same. Comparisons become pointless. Standings become irrelevant. There's no need for them.

So when I'm tempted to look around and see empty beer cans on the floor of someone's car or notice another person's habitual tardiness to church or get on the bullhorn to announce the mote I've spotted in someone's eye, I have to remind myself that Christ has made us equals. Nothing good about me makes me deserve salvation, and nothing bad about someone else makes him forfeit it. All my good deeds are a dirty pile of rags, and all my neighbor's wrong deeds are covered by the beautiful, pure robe of Jesus' righteousness.

In Christ we're free to simply love each other. Regardless of behavior. Regardless of personality or character. Regardless of "progress" in the Christian walk. Love takes the place of comparisons when Jesus removes the walls of hostility that separate us.

As a former math teacher, I sometimes like to use the idea of infinity. Of course, infinity really isn't a specific number. It's just an idea, an ethereal concept, as are a number of things in mathematics. Infinity is way out on the end of the number line, far past where you can count. You can't add to it. There's no such thing as infinity plus one. You couldn't have an infinite amount of money and then add just a little bit more. (That isn't to say I wouldn't be happy to try if given the chance!)

My point is that if two people both had an "infinity" of anything, you'd have to say they were equal in that regard. It would be pointless to do any comparing on the subject.

And in heaven, infinity will be a daily part of our lives. Do you ever wish you had more wealth? In heaven, you'll have an infinite amount of wealth—and so will everyone else.

So if down here you have $50 and you're discouraged because your neighbor has $500,000, don't despair over the financial comparison. In heaven his "infinity plus $500,000" and your "infinity plus $50" will be exactly the same. Again, the eternal life that Jesus provides makes us all equal.

I imagine that's one reason Jesus told the story referred to earlier in this book about the men who worked varying shifts, but all got paid the same. "Don't worry so much about who got paid what," He says. "Enjoy your own paycheck without casting glances at everyone else's to see who got some undeserved time-and-a-half. Remember, I've got an eternal life planned for each of you, with mansions and golden streets and pleasures that will make these puny paychecks fade into absolute insignificance."

In Christ, comparisons over finances or jobs or color or education or lifestyles or lifespan simply don't matter anymore. In heaven we'll all own the vast reserves of God's storehouse. We'll enjoy occupations that will thrill us with stimulation, challenge, and reward. We'll all be God's color, whatever that is. We'll all grow mentally for an eternity. We'll all experience lifestyles that meet our every dream. And we'll all live exactly the same length of time—forever.

Because of Christ, and because of His righteousness, and because of the eternal and infinite nature of the heaven He's preparing for us, we can be rid of the walls of hostility that divide us. We can be free to look at each other with eyes of love rather than with eyes of contrast.

I don't imagine the time will come soon when I can walk into San Diego's stadium in my Dodger Blue jacket and have fans welcome me with hearty hugs and exclamations of, "Welcome, brother!" And if anyone there offers me a 7-Up, I'll probably still be tempted to send it out for chemical analysis.

But I believe and pray that the time is coming when we who are Christians will at last put away our scorecards and our win-loss book of church standings. Someday soon, we will realize that we are all in first place together and that Jesus Christ is the One who won the all-important game that put us there.

Chapter 6
"It's This Cheap Glove!"

Here's a new sports term for you to learn: *mittsquinter*.

A mittsquinter is a person who makes an error in baseball and then immediately looks at his glove as if it were the guilty party.

Have you ever seen a mittsquinter? I sure have. In fact, my wife lives with one!

Next time you watch a game on TV, pay attention to the player who bobbles a grounder or has a fly ball kick off the heel of his glove. He'll never look at a teammate in the eye or even hang his head in shame.

No, he always glares at his glove, as if to say, "Why did you go and do that, especially on national TV? People might think it was *my* fault."

While he's at it, a mittsquinter probably mutters a few choice observations about the cows the leather came from and the factory workers who stitched the offending mitt together. Even the team equipment manager, who is certainly paid well enough that he ought to know how to buy decent gloves, must bear a portion of the guilt for the miscue.

I've seen balls go right between a shortstop's legs, where the ball doesn't come within six inches of the glove, and he still applies The Glare. "What's the matter with you? Why didn't you get down there and pick *that* one up?"

My favorite team, the Los Angeles Dodgers, seems to have gotten hold of a whole lockerful of bad gloves. I've even seen games where the entire team was wearing Brand X, and there

was an unbelievable rash of mittsquinting.

You'd think it would be a simple thing for someone in the front office to place a call to Ozzie Smith, the near-perfect shortstop from St. Louis, and say, "Listen, Oz, we want to know where you buy your gloves. I'm sending the whole team over."

Things are no better close to home. I play in a softball league every summer, and there are nights when my glove stinks up the whole joint. In a recent contest, with the game on the line, the batter hit a perfect double-play grounder right at me. I positioned myself correctly, placed my mitt right where the ball was supposed to go, and waited with calm expectation.

Somehow, the ball went right through my glove. To this day, I'm not sure if it was some flaw in my mitt, or if perhaps the ball, when it came off the assembly line at the factory, had some small irregularity that caused it to bounce erratically at that fateful moment. It's even possible that the dirt infield caused the mistake. Very likely the ball just didn't come up the way it should have because of an inconsistent playing surface.

Anyway, the ball went through my glove. That started a spate of five or six runs for the other team, and we lost the game. I was still busy squinting at my glove, the ball, and the uneven playing surface as my teammates trudged off the field. Later, in a merciless display of sarcasm, they voted me the game ball (probably defective), but gave me a croquet ball instead in honor of my outstanding performance as a wicket.

This mittsquinting phenomenon is also present in other aspects of the game. Batters strike out and immediately examine the bat quizzically, looking for air pockets. Baserunners get picked off and later accuse the pitcher and umpires of collusion to ignore blatant balks. A pitcher can have an ERA of 900 and walk in seven runs in a row, and then call a press conference to announce that the plate umpire was "pinching" him on ball-and-strike calls.

My favorite alibi story is from retired umpire Ron Luciano's great baseball book, *The Umpire Strikes Back*. He writes about Yankee Lou Piniella as an extremely argumentative player who has "successfully combined his hitting ability, his lack of speed and his fierce determination, to make himself into a truly terrible runner." On one occasion, Piniella managed to get himself thrown out at all four bases in a single game—"running for the cycle," as Luciano described it. He later added, "Years from now he'll probably be claiming the umpires were wrong on all four calls."

Other sports are just as susceptible to this cheap excuse-making. I play volleyball on Monday nights with a church group, and you should hear the alibis fly.

"This lopsided ball seems to always go sideways when I serve it."

"I couldn't find my Nikes. How can you expect me to cover any ground playing in my church shoes?"

"If I could get a decent set once in a while, I'd show you what a real power spike looks like."

"My wife didn't do the laundry yesterday. If I were wearing my new volleyball shorts, I'd never miss a simple shot like that one."

"What's the matter with this net anyway? It looks high to me. My serves don't usually go in the net like this."

On and on and on. Now some of my teammates are even starting to pick it up. With all the exercise we get passing the buck and dodging blame, you wouldn't think we'd have any energy left to play the game itself.

Of course, evading the painful truth about our frailties isn't limited to the playing field. Life is full of bobbing and weaving to avoid responsibility. Human nature is to see the good in ourselves, no matter how badly we must twist and distort our perceptions in order to do so.

I'm reminded of Bill Cosby's story about his late-night contests with his brother, to see who could jump higher on the bed. When the bed finally broke, and his father came charging down the hall and into the bedroom to investigate this assault on the family furniture, Bill was ready with a story.

"A man came in the window, Dad, and jumped on the bed. And . . . and . . . we told him 'You better not jump on the bed,

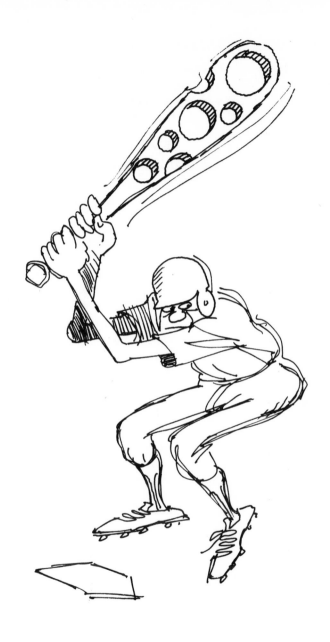

'cause it might break, and our dad will be mad,' but he just laughed at us. And . . . and . . . then the bed broke, and he climbed back out the window. Don't spank us, Dad."

"Window?" his dad thundered. "Window? This room hasn't got a window!"

"He brought the window with him, Dad," both boys wailed in unison. "Don't spank us, Dad."

"We Are Innocent." That's been the motto of the human race ever since the Garden of Eden, when Adam, clutching at his new fig-leaf trousers, suggested that God blame it on Eve. Eve, of course, blamed it on the serpent. I'm sure the serpent looked around frantically for another scapegoat to blame too.

"To err is human." Unfortunately, to *deny* our errors is also very human. Yet real spiritual growth cannot begin until we raise our hands and admit, "Perhaps I'm not so innocent after all." It's when I acknowledge that Romans 3:23—"All have sinned, and come short of the glory of God"—is talking about me, that I start to realize my need of a Saviour.

Someone once suggested that the five most important words in the English language are "I was wrong. I'm sorry." And history has shown over and over that God can do great things with a person who is willing to admit mistakes.

Great boulders in the path of matrimonial harmony can be removed. Badly bruised friendships can be repaired. Damaged relationships within God's family can be restored to wholeness.

All it takes is a person willing to say those five words: "I was wrong. I'm sorry."

Most important is the relationship with God that needs such careful attention, such watchful protection. Our most important apologies and confessions are the ones we make to Him.

That isn't to say God turns His back on us until we come crawling to Him with the magic phrase on our lips. Not for a minute! No, He waits patiently and eagerly, having already forgiven us even before we ask. It is for our sake that we must come to Him. He hasn't temporarily cast us off. We are still His children. Yet, how necessary and healing is that humble admission of guilt by the returning child: "Father, I made a mistake. I sinned against you. And I don't want my mistakes to ever damage the relationship I enjoy with you. Please forgive me."

And He replies, "Of course I do. In fact, I forgave you before you asked. But I'm glad you brought it up. I'm glad you care about our relationship, because I care about it too. And you're right in realizing that sin, unattended, could do great harm to our friendship. Thanks for working with Me to help protect that friendship. Now, let's get on with life together, shall we?"

The Bible tells the story of a great man who was willing to say, "I was wrong. I'm sorry." In fact, it is largely his repentance and resulting prayer for forgiveness that makes King David one of the greatest examples of a Bible champion.

It's especially difficult for kings and great leaders to admit mistakes, but King David does it with much humility in Psalm 51: "Have mercy upon me, O God, according to thy lovingkindness: according unto the multitude of thy tender mercies blot out my transgressions. Wash me thoroughly from mine iniquity, and cleanse me from my sin. For I acknowledge my transgression: and my sin is ever before me. . . . Purge me with hyssop, and I shall be clean: wash me, and I shall be whiter than snow. . . . Create in me a clean heart, O God; and renew a right spirit within me." Verses 1-10.

"I acknowledge my transgression." Courageous and noble words from a mighty king. And what an impact they had, not just in the life of King David himself, but for the entire nation he led.

"I was wrong. I'm sorry." Instead of squinting at our mitts or glaring at our bats, maybe we can instead look at ourselves as King David did. That's when we learn what our true condition really is. We discover, perhaps painfully, what kinds of ballplayers we really are.

"How good am I?" If we answer that one honestly, most of us will have to confess that what we really need is not better bats or a new equipment manager. No, what we need is a pinch hitter.

Something to think about.

Chapter 7
Thank You, Mr. Murphy

"If something can go wrong, it will."

Thank you, Mr. Murphy, for at least warning us.

This well-known adage was scientifically proved beyond the shadow of a doubt in a widely publicized bread-tossing experiment. Twenty slices of bread with butter and jelly were thrown into the air at random. Nineteen slices landed on the rug with the jelly-side down; the twentieth stuck to the ceiling.

A corollary to Murphy's Law was later added: "The tendency of bread to land with the jelly-side down is in direct proportion to the cost of the carpet."

Other scientifically developed bad news principles have recently been researched and published for the common good. Here are a few of the more helpful observations:

Balance's Law: The length of a minute varies according to which side of the bathroom door you're on.

Kovac's Conundrum: When you dial a wrong number, you never get a busy signal.

Bedfellow's Rule: The one who snores will fall asleep first.

Gold's Law: If the shoe fits, it's ugly.

Crane's Rule: There are three ways to get something done: Do it yourself, hire someone, or forbid your kids to do it.

My personal favorite, though, is entitled Moser's Law: "Exciting plays occur only while you are watching the scoreboard or out buying popcorn."

What I don't understand, though, is why it's called Moser's

Law. Who is this Moser fellow, anyway? I made this exact same observation *years* ago, based on season after season of personal experience. For all I know, Moser has never even been to a game, but just made up his law in order to get published.

It doesn't matter, I suppose, whose name is attached to the law. It's still one of the most meaningful observations ever penned about the game of baseball.

Moser's Law really is incomplete, however, unless you attach my personal Smith Amendment: "Home runs only occur when you're standing in line in the stadium restroom."

I'm not the least bit reticent about attaching my name to this eternal truth. I'm sure I have experienced this phenomenon at least as often as any other fan who ever loved the game. It never fails. I wait as long as I can before sprinting to the nearest restroom, but once I'm inside, the inevitable always happens. I hear a thunderous din echoing outside the walls. Wave after wave of cheers, or boos, fills the ballpark. And there I wait helplessly, cursing my consistent bad luck.

Even if I'm there for only two minutes, by the time I can dash back to my seat the excitement's completely over, the bases are empty, and a .195 hitter is at the plate with an 0-2 count on him and two outs.

"What happened? What happened?" My seatmate just shrugs and takes another bite of his ice cream sandwich. "Three-run homer by Marshall. Incredible moon shot. The ball landed about three rows from the back of the left field pavilion. Thought it was going to hit DiamondVision for a minute. I never seen such a long homer in my life."

"Why a *three-run* homer? Who got on base?"

"Oh, that. Stubbs hit one right under Rose's glove. Went down the line for a triple. It was great! Parker nearly had him at third, but they missed the tag. Then Guerrero got hit right in the back by a pitch. He almost went after Soto. I was sure a fight was going to break out. After everyone settled down, Marshall hit the first pitch for the homer. Couldn't you hear all the cheering?"

Thanks a lot, Mr. Moser.

I don't know how many Murphy laws I'm permitted to make up myself, but here's another one: "If you're late to a game, all the scoring will be in the first inning."

This is another surefire winner. Nothing makes me madder than to still be in the parking lot and hear frenzied roars coming from the stadium. And for some reason my wife seems to walk *slower* when we're late for a game than at any other time. "What's happening?" I shriek desperately at people jogging past me with radios plugged into their ears.

"Grand slam. Brock. Still nobody out."

I was on my way to a Mariners game in Seattle once when my wife made me late. She wanted me to get her something to eat first, if you can imagine that. Finally dropping her off at the motel, I drove three miles through downtown traffic to the stadium, fuming at every red light.

I missed just one and a half innings. The score was already 7-0. Minnesota had the bad manners to hit three home runs before I got to my seat.

The third rule of baseball is similar: "If you leave a game early, the team will achieve its season high in runs scored after you're out on the freeway."

A game can limp along 1-1 for seven innings, but just as soon as you get out to the parking lot, the stadium begins to rock. A friend of mine once left after eight innings just to "beat the traffic," with the home team up 2-1. Two hours later, his team finally prevailed 11-10 in twelve innings.

I've discovered, to my chagrin, that all three of these axioms apply equally to television. If a game begins at 4:30 p.m. and I don't get home until five, the score will already be eight to nothing. The minute the set warms up, I hear Vin Scully exclaim, "I've never seen an inning like this one in all my years of broadcasting!"

And I don't dare take a break that lasts longer than a Farmer John smoked ham commercial, either. I love my mother, but she has the thoughtless habit of calling long distance right during the seventh inning of deadlocked games. I give her baseball schedules to refer to, but she keeps losing them. I chat with her for ten or fifteen minutes, trying my best to sound amiable and relaxed. But my fears are invariably confirmed when I return to the game. Someone's always ahead by six runs.

I've discovered that the bad luck demons even invade video cassette recorders. A few years back I carefully set my VCR to tape a critical game while I attended an unavoidable meeting. My precious little two-year-old daughter, who doesn't have a malicious bone in her body, wandered by and noticed "all the pretty knobs."

I returned home three hours later and breathlessly turned on the tape. Three action-packed hours of—snow, accompanied by an unintelligible hum.

"If something can go wrong, it will." "Expect the unexpected." "Something big will always happen when you're not paying attention." Life is like that, isn't it?

The Bible offers a Murphy's Law that might be worth considering: "Be ye therefore ready also: for the Son of man cometh at an hour when ye think not." Luke 12:40.

It's interesting that Jesus tells us plainly: "I'll be coming at a time when you don't expect Me."

Christians all around the world look forward to Jesus' return. Along with John the Revelator, we pray, "Even so, Come, Lord Jesus." Revelation 22:20.

And the Bible gives so many clues that the time is near. Matthew 24 lists a number of signs to expect. Wars and rumors of wars. Earthquakes. Famines. False christs.

Bible students prepare detailed chronologies from the books of Daniel and Revelation that show clearly where we stand in earth's history. Evangelists pound their pulpits and announce that earth is in its final moments.

And yet, with all the warnings and the charts and the signs, we have this biblical Murphy's Law: Christ will come when least expected.

Why? I don't know. Many will "wax cold." Some will grow tired of waiting. Others will be deceived by false christs or counterfeit leaders. Many who trust in their powers of prophetic interpretation will be misled in one way or another.

There are a million ways to be wrong. There are plenty of

excuses for being unprepared. And Jesus warns us frankly that when He comes, it will be a surprise to most.

There's really only one way to be sure you're prepared, and that's to be ready all the time.

If I don't want to miss anything in baseball, I have to be there for the whole game. I can't come late. I can't leave early. And I can't afford to take time off in the middle to go buy popcorn.

It's appropriate for a Christian to watch for the warning signs and rejoice in what they reveal. It's commendable to study the Bible and the charts and the time lines. But the only security lies in constant preparedness. Constant surrender to God's will.

A relationship with Jesus Christ needs to be nurtured daily. It needs to be protected and guarded and fed on a constant basis. Abiding in Him is a twenty-four-hour job. Accepting and wearing His robe of righteousness is important enough, considering what's at stake, to warrant our full-time attention.

A distant cousin of Mr. Murphy once observed, "When my ship comes in, I'll probably be over at the train station."

Well, Mr. Murphy and Mr. Moser and their team of doomsayers may be right most of the time, but they don't have to be right in the end. If you're ready all the time, you'll be ready at the right time.

Chapter 8
The Empty House at Chavez Ravine

Let's talk about ballparks for a few minutes.

With all the excitement and drama surrounding a major league baseball game, it isn't often that a fan stops to notice the awesome physical structure that houses the game itself.

Baseball stadiums are impressive places. I don't care which one is your "home park." Next time you're there, take five minutes just to absorb the enormity of the place. The broad expanse of grass or Astroturf, the thousands of seats on several levels, the complex arrangement of concession stands, souvenir shops, restrooms, and other features.

Then, of course, there are the many parts of a ballpark that most of us rarely think about. The row of broadcasters' booths. The "Stadium Club" found in many parks. The clubhouses and runways. The security offices. Management suites. VIP boxes. All sorts of tunnels and elevators that ordinary people like you and me will never gain entrance to.

It's all so immense, complicated, and intriguing that I can't help but wish for an unhampered day to wander freely through it all.

Every park has its own features and complexities that make it unique. Candlestick Park in San Francisco, with its orange color scheme and multilayered dirt parking lots. Dodger Stadium's well-know yellow-orange-blue-red layers of seats, palm trees, and "sunken garden" effect in Chavez Ravine. Atlanta's Fulton County Stadium with the tepee out in the left field bleachers. Seattle's cavernous Kingdome with all of the flags hanging from the roof.

I'd love to spend a leisurely summer visiting all twenty-six stadiums, just to absorb the distinct flavor that each one has developed over the years. Boston's "Green Monster" left field wall. Houston's "Eighth Wonder of the World" Astrodome. Yankee Stadium, and all the history that ballpark holds. Wrigley Field's ivy-covered walls.

I propose a tip of the hat to the people who built these ballparks—men and women who had the vision, the know-how, and the business acumen to put such projects together.

Maybe I'm just easily impressed, but I'm frankly staggered by the enormity of such an undertaking. To plan and build a huge and intricate structure like Dodger Stadium is nothing short of a miracle in my estimation. I have great respect for people like that—people who dream big dreams and then accomplish them. Think of the men and women throughout the centuries who have committed their lives to the creation of architectural masterpieces. All the Empire State Buildings and Sistine Chapels and major league ballparks of the world stand as monuments to people with the gift of thinking and doing big things.

Others create masterpieces that are much smaller but no less incredible. Consider the world's great authors, for example, the great classic books, some of them hundreds and hundreds of pages in length, created with just a pen, an inkwell, and blank paper. No Apple IIe 128K word processors with find-and-replace or paragraph-swap functions. No IBM Selectric typewriters. No electronic WizardWriter aids of any kind. I can't even fathom the amount of work such a book represents.

As long as you're in the mood to be awestruck, how about the composers of ages present and past? The Mozarts, Beethovens, and Bachs of the world who created musical experiences that will never be forgotten. Again, you're talking about pen, inkwell, and hundreds of blank pages of manuscript paper turned into concertos, oratorios, sonatas, and grand symphonies.

I read once that Handel wrote his oratorio the *Messiah* in

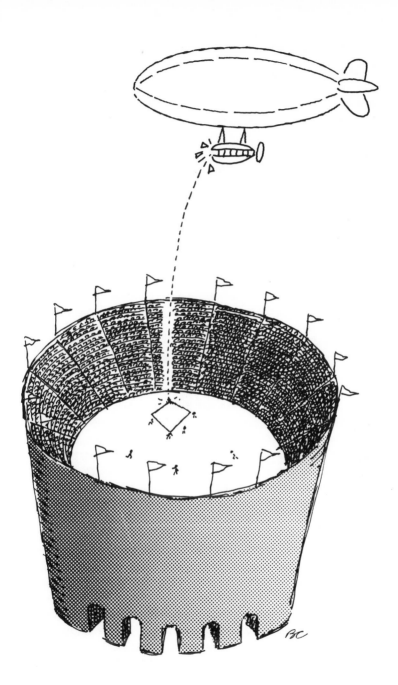

just twenty-four days, back in 1741. Twenty-four days! My well-worn Schirmer's edition runs 252 pages! That a composer could even mentally create such a work in 24 days, let alone set it all down note by note, is an unbelievable accomplishment.

Everywhere you look, no matter where you travel, the big achievements of big-dreaming people leap out at you. Buildings. Freeways. Widebody jets moving people here and there 500 at a time. Telecommunications systems tying the nation together via satellites.

And, in twenty-six major cities, the enormous concrete homes of America's favorite pastime.

But lest we become too absorbed in citing the collective achievements of mankind, let us turn our thoughts to this sobering reminder: A day is coming when major league ballparks will stand empty as tombs, never again to be filled. Silhouetted against the devastation of earth's final conflict, baseball parks and freeways and widebody jets will rest amid ruins with no one left on earth to occupy them or drive on them or fly in them.

Life here on earth seems so real, so permanent, at times. We're surrounded by things—houses, cars, clothes, ballparks—that are real and tangible. We can feel them, live in them, drive them.

What a challenge for us as Christians to keep our focus on the fact that heaven—often an intangible dream to us—is the reality we should be considering more. How often we need to be reminded that our "threescore and ten" here on earth, with all its material goods and human achievements, is soon to pass away so that the reality of heaven can begin at last! C. S. Lewis, in his book *Perelandra,* so aptly describes our brief life here on earth as a simple misstep or stumble that precedes the real journey, grand and glorious in its scope and adventure, that God intends us to experience.

There's nothing wrong with taking note of the accomplishments of great people. It certainly is God's plan that we live life to the full while we are here, taking advantage of all the benefits He has provided through His gift of creativity. But it may be well to regularly remind ourselves of the words of the old gospel tune:

> This world is not my home; I'm just a'passin' through.
> My treasures are laid up somewhere beyond the blue.
> The angels beckon me from heaven's open door,
> And I can't feel at home in this world anymore.

Chapter 9
Good News for Bob Uecker

Four no-hitters. 2,396 strikeouts. A .655 career win-loss record. A World Series ring. It's hard to argue with anyone who wants to call Sandy Koufax a legend. For several years in the 1960s he was one of the dominant forces in the game. The Los Angeles Dodgers built their winning strategy around him.

Opposing National League teams dreaded going to the ballpark if Koufax was going to be on the mound. Clubs always breathed a sigh of relief if they could manage to miss his spot in the rotation during a three-game set.

He was human, of course. Every now and then he lost a game just like anyone else. I lived overseas during most of the 1960s, so I had just one opportunity to see him pitch, during a visit to the United States in 1966. He got knocked out of the box in the fourth inning.

But bad outings were rare for Koufax. For most batters around the league, he was all but unhittable.

On another team was a young catcher named Bob Uecker. The word most often connected with his name was *mediocre*. His catching ability was suspect. Describing his technique for catching a knuckleball, Bob once said, "I just wait until it stops rolling, then pick it up." His batting average, year after year, hovered in the low 200s, and he hit so few career home runs that many fans can recall each one vividly.

There was a small knot of devoted but demented supporters, with tongues firmly planted in cheeks, who organized the Bob Uecker Fan Club. Surprisingly, the club was a great hit. Many joined up in an attempt to be funny or to establish their insanity for upcoming court cases.

The fan club's newsletter searched diligently for good news to print about Bob. Doctored statistics were presented which seemed to suggest that Uecker was actually a positive presence on the ballteam. "The team always wins whenever Bob catches the second game of twilight double-headers on the road on Thursdays," the club statistician would announce.

Members took great pains to view Uecker's attempts in the best possible light. With the bases loaded and one out, he would ground sharply into an inning-ending double play. "A clean shot," fans would declare. "A well-struck ball." "He got pretty good wood on that one." "If the second baseman had been playing three steps to his left that ball might have gone up the middle for a single." Etc.

Howard Cosell, on the other hand, tried to tell it like it is regarding Bob Uecker. "He stank."

Bob Uecker, by his own admission, played the game of baseball with such lack of flair that he has since built a whole new career out of appearing in "lite beer" commercials poking fun at his baseball abilities.

But there was one bright spot in this otherwise dismal career. One pitcher against whom Bob Uecker almost always had a field day: Sandy Koufax.

"I don't know the reason for it," Uecker admits. "But whenever Koufax pitched, I was certain to get hits. I'm sure Koufax was as baffled by it as I was."

Even though Koufax had the rest of the league "by the neck," he simply couldn't strike light-hitting Bob Uecker out. His masterful techniques were not effective in this one case.

Amazing baseball contributions sometimes come from the most unlikely sources. I've watched games where a pitcher who has gone 0 for 45 at the plate comes up with the bases loaded and hits a mammoth grand-slam home run. Or a second-string pitcher, number five in a five-man rotation, will inexplicably turn in a no-hitter.

I recall with bitter resentment how the '78 Yankees beat the Dodgers in the World Series four straight games. Most of

the damage was done by the two weakest Yankee hitters at the bottom of their lineup. Bucky Dent and Brian Doyle—and I still cannot say their names without involuntarily clenching my fists—hit .417 and .438 respectively. Revenge for Los Angeles came in 1981, however, when Steve Yeager, after a very anemic season, came up with a titanic game-winning homer in game five of the World Series.

It's funny how in a game dominated by the twenty-game winners and the triple crown hitters, it's often the little guys who make all the difference. Every player on the roster counts. Each member has a part to play, a role to fulfill.

The same is true in life. On a planet swarming with five billion people, a select few get most of the starring roles. Politicians. Celebrities. Sports heroes. Wealthy magnates. This is the crowd that seems to make the biggest impact shaping governments, building skyscrapers, writing novels, or making films that touch the lives of millions.

Yet there is a part for the rest of us to play as well. You have a role; I have a role. We each have a unique and valuable contribution to make.

Consider for a moment the one specific genetic combination that is you. There are literally billions of other combinations that could just as easily have occurred. But no, you are here because of that one unique blend, that single solitary meeting of egg and sperm.

I like to think that God ordained that meeting. Perhaps He surveyed the billions of possible combinations and then said, "This is the one. This particular union will give Me just the man or woman I need for a certain job down there on earth."

With that view in mind, I can thank Him for my gifts and live with my weaknesses. It's the way He planned it; He has a role for me to fulfill with the specific strengths and limitations built into this human package.

And what of human worth? If you and I are chosen by God, what does that say of our value? Are we not an immeasurable treasure to Him?

"I'm a child of the King," we sing. That establishes some sort of a price tag, doesn't it? Jesus talked about sparrows, describing the Father's love for them, and then asserted, "Ye are of more value than many sparrows." Luke 12:7.

I read once that Christ would have come to this earth to die for just one sinner who needed the gift of salvation. That says a great deal about the worth of an individual, even those most ordinary or inept.

Good news indeed for Bob Uecker. And also for you and for me.

Chapter 10
Goose Bumps

What gives a person the "goose bumps," anyway? Aside from a late-evening walk without a sweater, I mean. What kinds of emotional experiences affect you to the point where you actually have a physical reaction of some kind?

It's interesting to observe how different people react in completely opposite ways to the same emotional circumstances. I remember taking my sixth-grade class to a dramatized version of *The Miracle Worker*, the story of Helen Keller's childhood. At the grand climax of the play, Helen finally grasps the concept that language has meaning. She realizes for the first time that she has found a door of communication that will allow her to reach out to the world.

The finale of the play was so moving, so absolutely spellbinding in its forcefulness, that I was emotionally overcome by it. I sat motionless in my seat, tears streaming down my face. I looked across the aisle and noticed that our principal, a big athletic man, was also blubbering like a baby.

My students, on the other hand, sat there like twenty stony lumps. I mean, they had hearts of *concrete*. I felt like flunking every one of them, but, of course, you can't mark kids down just because their hearts and tear ducts don't function properly.

Please don't get the idea that I'm a complete baby. I just have a very specific list of life experiences that "get to me" without fail.

Take funerals, for example. I get emotional at funerals.

Anybody's funeral. I've been to services for someone I've never even met, and just seeing the deceased person's relatives there will cause me to get misty-eyed. Feelings of sympathy, I suppose.

Other things never fail to move me in a truly positive way. For example, Martin Luther King, Jr.'s famous "I Have a Dream" speech. I've seen it on film on seven or eight occasions and have had to dab at my eyes each time.

The "Hallelujah Chorus" from Handel's *Messiah* is another five-star winner. For a number of years our church presented it every year at Christmas, and I had the privilege of directing the choir. As those absolutely inspired lyrics—"King of kings and Lord of lords!"—and majestic chords enveloped me, I would get so emotional I could hardly see my music.

And it didn't just affect me at performances. I'd get goose bumps even at rehearsals, or when I played it on the stereo at home—even while standing in the shower directing an imaginary choir of thousands. That music simply does a number on me every single time.

Then, of course, there are those emotional experiences that typically strike a chord in almost any person. Weddings, for example. I was probably not that unique in feeling a special tingle on my wedding day that I won't ever forget.

Witnessing the birth of my own child is another emotion-laden memory. Seeing at first just a sliver of my baby's scalp, and then suddenly watching a head emerge and seeing those little eyes, nose, and mouth—that's really something. I wanted to cry out, "Lord, it really is a baby! We made a human being!" Not that I expected something else, but the reality of this miracle of creation stopped me dead in my tracks. To have something that for nine months was simply "the baby" now become transformed into my living, breathing, tiny daughter was a heartstopper that rated a "10" on my list of emotional highs.

I mentioned my emotional reaction to a friend who had had the same experience a few weeks earlier, just to see if my response was typical. He looked at me soberly and replied, "I thought my heart would stop." So I guess I'm normal.

BOB CRAM

After such reverent reminiscing, I hope it isn't close to sacrilege to draw additional illustrations from the wide world of sports. Any honest American fan will admit that there are moments when the thrill of victory brings the goose bumps and the moist eyes along with the victor's cup.

I suppose every fan has his favorite. Forty-Niner Dwight Clark's playoff catch against the Cowboys. Reggie Jackson's three home runs for the Yankees in the final game of the 1977 World Series. (I thought I would die. What a dreadful evening.) The 1980 U.S. victory in hockey at Lake Placid. Boston's comeback in game five of the '86 baseball playoffs— another black day for West Coast fans.

My personal favorite happened in September 1983. It was Dodgers vs. Atlanta at Dodger Stadium with two weeks left in the season.

The Dodgers were in first place, nursing a two-game lead over the Braves, so the outcome of this game meant a volatile two-game swing in the standings. They could be either up by a robust three games or a mere one.

In other words, the universe was on the line.

Things were going along nicely, with a Dodger 2-1 lead, when Dale Murphy upset the apple cart with one swing. It was a three-run homer from the moment it left his bat.

I sat there with my head in my hands for a couple of innings, looking up only whenever a Braves hitter got a base hit, which was every fifteen seconds or so for what seemed an eternity. Before the dust settled, we were looking up from a 6-3 deficit with just one inning to go.

The 50,000 fans were mostly in the parking lot and on the freeway by this time, but not me. (I was with someone else, and we were using his car.) "Never say die!" I asserted, trying to inject some optimism into my voice.

"It's not over till the fat lady sings," shouted a rather obese woman sitting behind us as she pulled some sheet music out of her handbag.

With the pitcher due to lead off the bottom of the ninth, manager Tommy Lasorda sent up pinch-hitter Jose Morales to bat in his spot. "Come on," I mumbled to myself. "Make that pitcher work. Draw a walk, man, draw a walk."

Jose swung weakly at the first pitch. Almost a one-handed swing. I groaned and kicked at the seat in front of me.

The ball sailed into the left-field corner for a double.

Steve Sax came up and walked on four pitches.

Suddenly, a glimmer of hope began to well up within me. The tying run coming to the plate? No outs? Could it possibly be?

"Put away that music," I instructed the fat lady. "We still got a shot."

Bill Russell, who hits home runs only on any June 31 that's the sixth Sunday of the month, came to the plate. "Time for a miracle," I howled, rising to my feet. He struck out weakly. One away.

I sat back down.

Dusty Baker came to the plate. He hit a high fly ball to right center that somehow managed to find that one corridor of airspace no fielder could get to. "That one's trouble!" announcer Vin Scully shouted. "It's going to *drop!*"

Drop it did, and the bases were loaded. Still just one out, and the Big Guy coming to the plate. Everyone stood up again.

Pedro Guerrero. Capable of hitting a home run any day of the year. One grand-slam swing and the game is over, I thought.

Not this time. The count built up to three and two. The entire stadium, all 20,000 remaining faithful fans, were screaming by now. It was Nun Day at Dodger Stadium, and there were black-robed sisters all over the place. One little old Spanish Mother Superior behind me was shrieking with the best of them, fingering her beads with fervor.

"Keep on praying, Sister," we urged.

"I will, I will," she promised tearfully, in her broken English.

With the count still full, Pedro fouled off three successive pitches. "He just *did* get a piece of that one," Scully kept repeating from his broadcasting booth. "What tension! What a game!"

Finally the big pitch. Ball four.

That brought in a run. Now it was 6-4 with the tying run out there at second. "Just a base hit ties it up," we chanted endlessly.

Mike Marshall looked at two balls, then jumped on a pitch high and outside. And drove it to the wall in right and over the fielder's head. Two runs scored on the opposite-field double. I was so sure Pedro would score from first on the play that I began celebrating too soon. The base coach had held him at third! We were tied at six, but a victory was still ninety feet away.

The stadium was rocking with emotion that you had to see to believe. Everybody on his feet. Nonstop clapping. Pleading for just one more base hit.

With first base open, the Braves walked Greg Brock intentionally, bringing R. J. Reynolds, a rookie, to the plate.

Then it happened. It will probably be the single most memorable at-bat R. J. will ever have. Years later, Braves announcers on Atlanta's superstation, WTBS, still refer to it every time the Braves pitch to him.

"*THE SQUEEZE IS ON!*" Scully shouted. I could almost hear him direct from the radio booth. "*And here comes the run!*"

R. J. laid down the bunt to perfection. Guerrero, who was breaking with the pitch, crossed the plate without a play.

Pandemonium.

In the midst of the ensuing excitement, I looked at my watch. We had been on our feet clapping for twenty-five solid minutes. My hands were aching. My voice was gone. But I was buoyed up by an emotional impact that I remember to this day.

Later, in the relative solitude of my home, I reflected on the thrill of victory we had experienced that day. The goose bumps came back as I relived the emotional high of that final play.

Then my mind skipped ahead to a day yet to come. A day when we'll see a very special cloud coming in the skies, and a very special King coming to take us home with Him.

How will we feel, I wonder? What emotions will we experience when it begins to sink in that the great controversy

of the universe is finally over and we are on the winning side? We can only imagine. Yet the Bible assures us that our imaginations are totally inadequate to paint the picture properly.

I don't know how I'll react when I realize that the long-awaited time has finally arrived. How I'll respond to the realization that life in God's eternity is about to begin.

I do know this. I'll experience a wellspring of emotion that will overshadow Dodger games and Hallelujah Choruses and live births and weddings. You'd better believe it!

I may shout a little. I may sing praises. I may just stand there for hours with my arms outstretched and tears streaming down my face, not wanting to miss one moment of this glorious and precious experience. And I'll tell you this too: I don't plan to miss it. I like being excited. I savor the thrill of victory. I don't even mind standing in the middle of a crowd with tears streaming down my cheeks.

I bet you won't either.

Chapter 11
You Root for the *Cardinals?*

Here's a chapter for everyone who lives in Missouri or Massachusetts.

It was game six of the National League Championship Series between the Dodgers and the St. Louis Cardinals. Top of the ninth, Dodgers leading by one, but the Cards had men on second and third with two out and slugger Jack Clark coming to the plate.

Decision time. Do you pitch to Clark or walk him intentionally and take your chances with the next batter?

My theory is this: don't let yourself get beat by Mr. Big. Clutch home run hitters have a bad habit of hitting clutch home runs.

Unfortunately, Tom Lasorda was not taking phone calls at that moment, and he directed Tom Niedenfuer to pitch to Clark.

Clark deposited the first pitch in the left field pavilion and the entire '85 season turned to ashes.

Needless to say, I was devastated. For several hours I just walked around in a daze, trying to find a fairly thin wall I could put my fist through.

But here is the startling thing: *people in Missouri were actually HAPPY that Clark hit that homer.*

Can you comprehend such a thing? Residents of St. Louis were celebrating this heartbreaking turn of events. They were glad that the Dodgers lost!

Imagine. Normal people just like me, who go to work each

day, and who lead responsible lives and feed their pets faithfully, were rooting for Clark to hit the ball out and dash my team's hopes.

In fact, during the entire playoffs, those people were taking the absolute *opposite* viewpoint from mine on every single play. Every time I mumbled to myself, "Come on, baby, just a base hit," they were chanting, "Strikeout. Strikeout. Strikeout." And when the teams switched sides, all the fans would too. Now it was me going, "Fan 'em, fan 'em, fan 'em," while Missourians were rooting for the hit parade to begin.

Think of it. Decent Christian folks in Missouri and decent Christian folks in Los Angeles, and all of them hoping for the exact opposite thing to happen. What kind of a world is that?

Same thing in basketball. Just the other day the L.A. Lakers beat the Boston Celtics in six games to take the '86 title. I happened to be in California for a series of speaking engagements and had the opportunity to visit an avid basketball fan. Turns out he was a loyal supporter of the Celtics!

I couldn't even imagine such a thing. How could he root for the *Celtics*? How could he hope that Bird and McHale and Parish and, especially, Ainge, would actually make baskets? Unthinkable!

Watch an L.A.-Boston championship game on TV, and you'll see a whole stadium full of people at the Boston Garden—and the funny thing is that they all want Boston to win! Every fan there is rooting for the exact opposite result that I'm looking for in every single play!

On every foul called, they want "block" when I want "charge." On every shot attempted, they want "swish" when I want "No good—and Magic's got the rebound for a fast break." On every pass attempted, they want "Score!" when I want "Intercepted!"

There's a very simple lesson here: *there are other viewpoints besides mine in this world.*

That's a concept that's ever so easy to forget, and humbling to remember! And every time I square my jaw and plant my feet in cement, I remember those Cardinal fans and the Celtics diehards, and I try to keep in mind that others may see things just a bit differently than I do.

Every four years when I step into a voting booth to help select a president, I'm reminded in very clear terms that millions of normal Americans view some things from a different perspective than mine! No matter how convinced I am that *my* vision for America is the right one, I have to make room for these diverse opinions.

I find the same thing at work. As a member of our company's "house committee," I frequently find that several perspectives are better than one. Sometimes my most fervent convictions are drastically altered by other people's overwhelmingly sound viewpoints.

The older I get the more I realize that I'm not always right! Sometimes someone else is right instead.

Try this experiment with me: count the number of "f's" in the following sentence:

Feature films are the result of years of scientific study combined with many years of experience.

That's it. No trick question. No hidden meaning. Just count those "f's."

How many did you find?

If you try this with a large group, you'll discover something very interesting: different ones will be *absolutely convinced* that there are three f's, four f's—even as many as six f's. Several answers—and every person in the group will raise his hand to testify that he *knows* he has the right one.

Only when faced with incontrovertible evidence of their error will the mistaken counters admit they were wrong. Some even find that difficult! A friend of mine tried this experiment at a workshop, noted the varying reactions, and then revealed the right answer (six). *Two months later,* he received a lengthy and fairly heated letter from one of the attendees, still claiming that his answer of "four" was the right one!

"There are viewpoints other than mine." That perspective is especially important in dealing with fellow Christians in matters of religion.

I feel privileged to have many opportunities to associate with Christians of different faiths. For some months I enjoyed serving as the pianist for a church other than my own. I've given countless parenting seminars at churches of many denominations. I've attended workshops where men and women from many religious backgrounds were present. And each encounter has broadened my appreciation for the sincerely held viewpoints of others.

Don't get me wrong. I love my church. I appreciate what I perceive to be the soundness of its beliefs. I believe that in these last days God will so direct the events of this world that people will have an opportunity to make very clear decisions about those beliefs that are necessary to salvation.

Having said that, let me suggest that one of the most delightful things about heaven will be the many discoveries we will make concerning things we might have been wrong about! Pastor Jerry Cook, in his wonderful book *Love, Acceptance, and Forgiveness,* describes saints who are on the cloud on their way to heaven, still referring to their prophetic charts and time lines, protesting, "Wait a minute! My chart says we should still be doing such-and-such."

The bottom line is, we'll be glad we're on our way to heaven, with an eternity before us where we can hear all the correct answers from God Himself.

I just want to be there, don't you? I can agree with *anybody* on that. Even a Larry Bird fan.

Chapter 12
Too Busy Watching Gilligan's Island

A few weeks ago I took my four-year-old daughter, Karli, to a baseball game. Dodgers vs. Expos. I'm trying to bring her up right, you see.

For days before the big event, she told everybody about her upcoming night of fun. "I'm going to a ballgame with my daddy," she proudly informed all her little playmates at pre-school.

Of course, I had carefully coached her on all the proper etiquette associated with attendance at a major league baseball game: how to yell "CHARGE!" when the stadium organ plays the appropriate fanfare; how to boo the umpire after a bad call; how to throw confetti on spectators sitting one level below after a Dodger home run; how to get down on one's knees and pound the ground in frustration after a bases-loaded-nobody-out situation goes down the drain; etc.

So she was all set for a great night out with Dad. Just the two of us. She got dressed up just as cute as can be in a little Dodger T-shirt, and away we went.

She had a fantastic time. My wife had packed a great sack lunch for us, and Karli happily gobbled down all her food and half of mine. Then she wanted popcorn. And an ice cream "samwich." And soda. And peanuts. All through the game she cheerfully munched on everything Daddy said yes to—which was everything.

And it was "ball night," too! All youngsters fourteen and younger received a free major league baseball courtesy of the

BOB CRAM

Dodgers. I tried to get one for myself, but even though I was wearing a hat with a little propeller on it to add to my youthful appearance, the concession girl didn't fall for it. "Come on, you're over fourteen," she chided.

"That's right," my precious daughter chimed in. "My daddy's thirty-two!"

Oh well. At least I got to play with Karli's ball. In fact, I got to handle it quite a bit during that game. "Here, Daddy, hold my ball while I eat my samwich." "Daddy, can I have my ball back now?" "Here, Daddy, I'm tired of holding it." "Daddy, let me play with it again." "Daddy, I dropped it." "Daddy, why is that man holding his head and shouting at us?" And so on.

Other entertainment at the game included the big Dodgervision television scoreboard screen, the traditional seventh-inning sing-along of "Take Me Out to the Ballgame," and a little boy sitting right behind us who entertained my daughter by dropping peanut shells on my head during most of the game.

And I must mention that the game was punctuated by numerous trips to the stadium restrooms. Every time the Dodgers had the bases loaded, Karli had to go.

All in all, it was a great evening. An experience to delight the senses. And for three fun-filled hours my daughter took in each and every sensory treat . . . except one.

The game itself.

The actual contest down on the field meant absolutely nothing to her. One to nothing, twenty-eight to twenty-seven—it wouldn't have made any difference to her. The ballgame we had driven forty-five miles to watch was the one thing that held no fascination for Karli. In her delight over ice cream samwiches and free baseballs, she missed the game.

Well, no big deal. Come to think of it, considering the final score—Expos 3, Dodgers 1—I almost wished I had missed it myself.

Yet, there are times when missing out on what ought to be a not-to-be-missed experience has more sobering implications.

Think back with me to a Thursday evening nearly two thousand years ago. The Garden of Gethsemane. Jesus is with His three closest earthly friends: Peter, James, and John. Do you remember the scene? It was a night of untold agony for Christ. Despair such as you and I simply cannot imagine overwhelmed Him as He struggled alone with the burden of this world's sin and the knowledge of what lay ahead. Luke says that Jesus struggled with such intensity that His sweat was "as it were great drops of blood falling down to the ground." Luke 22:44.

And is it any wonder? That weekend was the climax of the centuries-long struggle between Christ and Satan. The "great controversy," as many refer to it, was coming to a head. And Jesus knew full well that the fate of this planet rested with Him. His lonely decision that evening about tomorrow's Calvary carried eternal implications for the future of God's government.

What a moment!

Meanwhile, Jesus' three faithful friends, Peter, James, and John, were sleeping like babies. The struggle of the ages was happening just a few feet away, yet they weren't able to stay awake—even after repeated requests from their Saviour who needed them so desperately.

They were right there, and they missed it!

The next afternoon the same tragic scene was repeated. Christ, the crucified Lord, was lifted up on a cross before a watching throng. Holy, unfallen beings on other worlds watched in silence as Jesus won the battle that spelled victory in that great controversy against evil that had gone on for so long. At the foot of the cross during these climactic scenes was a small group of Roman soldiers. And what were they doing as the greatest victory ever achieved was accomplished? Casting lots for His coat! Just inches away, their Saviour hung on a cross, winning their eternal freedom with His sacrifice, and those poor, dumb soldiers were too busy with a dice game to notice.

Matthew 27:36 tells it all with seven poignant words: "And sitting down they watched Him there."

What a tragedy! To be right there and still miss everything.

How about today, my friend? As events on this worn-out planet spin down to their final conclusions, is it possible that

we could miss out as well?

One day very soon now, Jesus our King will return to this earth in triumph, in a rescue mission for those who have gone to the effort to get to know Him as a Friend.

What a tragedy it would be to be right there, a member of the last generation, and yet miss out. To be caught unprepared. To be left behind because we had never bothered to spend that necessary time each day drawing close to the soon-returning King.

Don't let it happen to you.

I wish I could come over to your house, wherever you are, as you read these words, and say it to you face to face: *"Don't let it happen to you. Make Jesus Your Friend today."* I wish you could encourage me the same way. I need it, too, you see. I need to have friends remind me that we *can* make it! Be prepared! Be there!

I often tease my wife Lisa about her lukewarm interest in baseball. "I bet if I was out of town on business during game seven of the World Series and called you during the middle of the ninth inning, I'd catch you watching 'Gilligan's Island' instead," I chided her one day. "The greatest moment in all of sports, and you'd be on the wrong channel."

Let me say it to *you*. One of these days it won't be the World Series. It will be the *world*. Game seven. And I want you to be there. Tuned in to God's channel.

Chapter 13
To the Track . . . To the Wall . . . It's Gone!

Vin Scully was the sports announcer on Los Angeles' KABC radio. It was game five of the 1981 World Series, Dodgers vs. Yankees, bottom of the seventh. The Yankees were leading 1 to 0, with Ron Guidry pitching to Dodger powerhitter Pedro Guerrero.

"Now the strike-one pitch to Pedro Guerrero," Scully entoned over the mike. He almost sounded bored. Suddenly his voice changed. You could almost see Scully leap to his feet in front of the mike: "Breaking ball, a high fly ball to left! Back goes Piniella (the left fielder) . . . it's gone!" Pedro Guerrero had hit a home run into the bleachers.

"A one-to-one tie," Scully exulted over the mike. "Guerrero's getting a bear hug from Tommy Lasorda, and this crowd wants Guerrero to come out on the field. They're cheering for Guerrero. They're pleading for Guerrero. And here he comes!"

Guerrero was just starting to come up the steps from the dugout when he saw that Guidry was pitching to Yeager, and he went back down.

"O-and-one the count to Yeager," Scully continued from the radio booth. "The strike-one pitch in the dirt. Down in the Yankee bullpen they begin to move around. Guidry squinting into Cerone (the catcher)."

Now Scully's voice coming over the radio sounded tense. Excited. "The one-two (sic) pitch to Yeager. Swung on . . ." and suddenly you'd have thought Scully was going to burst out of his radio booth onto the field. "*Another high drive! Back*

89

Piniella, way back—it's gone!"

Nothing quite equals the excitement of a radio announcer's home-run call in baseball. It's either thrilling or devastating, depending on what color pennant you happen to be waving. Announcers develop an especially distinctive style in calling a homer. Scully is one of the best in the business. His description of the Yeager homer was vintage Vinnie: "Back goes Piniella . . . awaaaaay back . . . *it's gone!"*

Whether you're rooting for the good guys or the bad guys, no one can deny that a home run is one of the most potent, exciting plays in the game. A surprising number of games hinge on that one key blow.

Tom Lasorda, Dodger manager for many years, has a magic formula he quotes to his team: "3RH + WPG = PENNANT. Translated: Three-run homers plus well-pitched games = pennants."

Almost any game can be dramatically affected by a good three-run home run. If you're already up by two, that three-run blast effectively blows the game wide open. But even if you're down by five or six runs, a three-run shot puts you right back in the thick of things.

Of course, a grand slam is . . . well, a grand slam—even when it's for the opposition. What more can I say?

I was in a jam-packed Candlestick Park one day when Mike Ivie of the Giants hit a grand slam against L.A. Do you have any idea what kind of roar 56,999 San Francisco fans make at a time like that? Believe me, that wall of sound is magnified a thousand times when you're the only one in the stadium sitting there in stunned silence.

Two innings later, it should be pointed out, Reggie Smith of the Dodgers hit a two-run homer to tie the game back up. Now it was time for those 56,999 fans to sit quietly and listen to me cheer all by myself!

It's interesting to note how the home ballpark treats "home" homers as compared to "visitor" homers. At Dodger Stadium the organ plays a little fanfare and then a drum roll for an L.A. blast. A visitor homer, on the other hand, is quietly put up on the scoreboard in dead silence.

The Chicago White Sox, in years gone by, have been one of the most blatantly one-sided teams in their tributes to the long ball. A Chicago home run was honored by an exploding scoreboard, complete with fireworks, smoke, light displays, and a thundering rendition of "The Hallelujah Chorus" blaring from every loudspeaker, along with a little theme music from the Lone Ranger thrown in for free.

But for a visitor home run? The silence was deafening.

One visiting team, so the story goes, decided that enough was enough. After several fireworks displays for Chicago runs, one of their own players also hit one out. The scorekeeper dutifully put a 1 up on the board. The visiting manager gave a signal to his players and they silently filed out onto the field to face the crowd. In the fascinated silence that followed, the players each lit a sparkler and waved it desperately at the hostile home folks.

But enough folklore. What's the point?

Simply this. A home run is the one offensive play that's a sure thing. A home run is instant money in the bank. That's not true of any other play, no matter how promising it may appear. Only a home run comes with guaranteed results.

A batter may hit a long triple with nobody out. Everybody in the ballpark may be absolutely convinced that the home team will somehow bring him in. But until the player actually crosses the plate, it doesn't count.

I can painfully remember many games where my team had that winning run on third base with nobody out in the bottom of the ninth. Victory lay just ninety feet away. Surely they couldn't blow it this time! There were a million ways to get that player home: base hit, sacrifice fly, squeeze bunt, wild pitch.

Yet time and time again that "sure thing" turned out to be not so sure after all. Bases loaded, nobody out, winning run coming down the line from third. Then pop-up, strikeout, harmless fly ball, and before you could say "choke," the inning was over.

Not so with the home run. The minute it crosses the out-field fence, no one can stop that player from crossing over the plate. A home run is a sure thing.

I remember an L.A.-Houston game that went to fourteen innings. This game had everything: seesaw leads, lead-off triples that never scored, pitchers getting out of bases-loaded-nobody-out jams, diving catches to save a sure double.

The Dodgers scored twice in the top of the twelfth. "This is it!" I exulted to my sleeping wife. "My patience has been rewarded."

Houston came right back with two in the bottom of the inning. On to the thirteenth we went.

The Dodgers used up so many players that the manager actually had to bring in a pitcher from the outfield. In the bottom of the thirteenth Houston got a runner to third with only one out. In a master stroke of genius, Lasorda had Bob Welch, the pitcher-turned-outfielder, switch places with Dusty Baker, the regular strong-armed outfielder. Sure enough, the next batter hit a ball right to Baker, who threw out the runner from third trying to score the winning run on a sacrifice fly.

Then, after almost five hours of missed chances, strategic moves, intrigue, and counterattacks, Jose Cruz quietly hit a home run in the bottom of the fourteenth and the game was instantly over. Just like that. The home run was the only sure thing.

Few things in life are as sure as a homer. Most of the time, about all we get is that lead-off triple: a man on third base and a whole lot of hoping.

But thank God, some things do come guaranteed. His sure things are money in the bank.

Take Christ's sacrifice on the cross, for example. When Jesus died, the ball game was over. Praise God, that's one home run that can never be called back.

"It is finished!" He cried. And He was right. The great controversy was resolved that day. Christ was declared Victor. And a watching universe agreed.

I'm so glad that Christianity is not based merely on hope, or on wishful thinking. Good as it may look, our security isn't based on a runner on with no outs. No, the ball has already sailed out of the park. The score has already been posted! It's written in the Bible: Jesus won! And His victory is ours.

Another eternally sure thing is the home-run security we can enjoy in our assurance of salvation. My favorite Bible text describes this very assurance: "I write these things to you who believe in the name of the Son of God so that you may *know* that you have eternal life." 1 John 5:13, NIV. Italics mine.

Not hope. Not wishful thinking. Not, "We need just one more base hit to bring that runner home from third!"

No, the run has scored already, and it's a home run! We can know that our salvation is secure. We simply abide daily in the One who has already won our victory for us.

Dodgers vs. Phillies, May 1981. The game had been close all the way. The score stood tied at two after nine innings. With two outs and the bases empty in the bottom of the tenth, Rick Monday rocketed a home run into the right-field pavilion. Just like that, the game was over and the fans, savoring the sweet feelings of exultation and contentment, began filing out to the exits.

I lingered for just a moment, enjoying the quiet night air and the feeling of being part of the victory. The home run was good. The run was home. Nobody could take it away. It felt great.

That's how Christians can feel all the time.